The Adventures of Ja Ja and Jamila
GOING TO AFRICA

WRITTEN BY NEHANDA GREEN

ILLUSTRATED BY FRANCENE WARNER

EDITED BY GLORIA HOUSE

The Adventures of JaJa Series
KEIRA PRESS LLC

The Adventures of JaJa and Jamila Going to Africa
Copyright 2009
Keira Press LLC

The Adventures of JaJa Series Book 1

Library of Congress Control Number: 2009904324

ALL RIGHTS RESERVED
No portion of this publication may be reproduced,
stored in any electronic system, or transmitted in any form or
by any means, electronic, mechanical, photocopy, recording, or otherwise,
without written permission from the author.
Brief quotations may be used in literary reviews.

ISBN: 978-0-9824506-0-4
First printing: May 2009

FOR INFORMATION CONTACT:
KEIRA PRESS LLC
P.O. Box 815
Joliet, IL 60434
815.726.4200
Please visit our web site at
www.keirapress.com
Online ordering is available

Printed in the USA
MAYS PRINTING COMPANY, Inc.
15800 Livernois Avenue, Detroit, Michigan 48238
313.861.1900
www.maysprinting.com

CONTENTS

Dear Journal 1

Getting Ready to Go Is Hard Work! 3

Africa, Here We Come! 7

Touchdown in Banjul! 11

Our Host Family 13

The Garden 17

Shopping at the Tourist Market 19

Getting Around in Gambia 23

Buying Presents for Everyone 25

What's a Good Price for Fish? 27

The Tailor Shop on the Front Porch 29

Watch Out for Mosquitoes! 31

Gambian Friends 33

Lights On, Lights Off 35

One Ocean, Two Coasts 37

Ms. Mariamme Takes Us to School 39

Show and Tell 43

Time to Go Home 45

Dear Journal: The Long Trip Back 47

The Adventures of JaJa and Jamila Going to Africa

# THE ADVENTURES OF JAJA AND JAMILA GOING TO AFRICA

DEAR JOURNAL:

My name is Jamila. I live with my mother, father and little sister, Yanni, in a midwestern city. I am in the sixth grade and attend school near my house. I walk to school with my two best friends, Oni and Njoki, who live around the corner. They are twins. Most people can't tell the two of them apart, but I can. They sometimes like to play tricks on people and make them think they are not who they are.

My grandmother -- we call her JaJa -- lives very near me. She is my mother's mother. JaJa means grandmother in a language from East Africa. I wanted you to know a little about my family before I tell you the really good news. I'm going on my first trip overseas! I am going to Africa with JaJa. We are going to a country named Gambia in West Africa.

JaJa is chairperson for an organization called the Concerned Citizens for World Education (CCWE). This organization raises money to educate children living in Africa and other parts of the world, whose families can't afford the fees to send them to school. The CCWE gives scholarships to children between the ages of four and seventeen. Because JaJa is the chairperson of the CCWE, she was asked to go to Gambia to evaluate the program's progress, collect all of the students' information, and get current photographs of the scholarship children.

My grandmother had often told me she would take me to Africa with her. I had asked her many times if I could go to Africa with her. She would always say, "Not now -- maybe next time." This time I asked her again and she said yes!

JaJa said she had already asked my parents and they said yes. She said it was going to be fun to meet new children living in another part of the world. I was so excited I could not wait to leave on our trip. I told everyone I was going. I told Oni and Njoki, everyone at school and church, and everyone in the neighborhood.

GETTING READY TO GO IS HARD WORK!

Before we could go on our trip, there were quite a few things that had to be done. First JaJa took me to the neighborhood store to have photographs taken of me for my passport and visa. The store clerk took my picture with a digital camera while I stood in front of a screen with a white background. It reminded me of a small movie screen. The store was not busy, so it only took a few minutes to develop the pictures. JaJa purchased 10 prints, two for the passport, two for the visa and a few extras. JaJa said anything could happen while we were away and we might need extra pictures. As an example, she explained that if I lost my passport, I would need extra photos to have it replaced.

Before anyone is permitted to leave this country going overseas and before anyone is allowed to enter another country, they have to have a passport. JaJa has had a passport for many years because she travels outside the country a lot. The United States federal government issues passports.

In order to get your passport, you need to complete an application. In my case, my parents completed the application for me because I am a minor. I had to have two recent small photos of myself, my birth certificate, proof of my current address, and permission from my parents (because I am a minor). Then JaJa took me to the post office to be interviewed. Finally, we had to pay the passport fee.

Everything went smoothly. My passport arrived in the mail in about ten weeks. It has my picture, name, date of birth, where the passport was issued, when the passport was issued, when it expires and my passport number.

After my passport arrived, we needed visas from the African country we are going to visit. To receive the visas, we went on line to the web site of Gambia and printed the visitor applications. My parents filled out the application for me and mailed it to the Gambian Embassy in Washington, D.C. We had to include with the application our passports, two current pictures of ourselves, the visa fees and a self-addressed, stamped return envelope. When the visas were approved and returned, I was really happy. My visa is in my passport and is good for a year. It allows me to visit Gambia within a certain time period and stay for a certain length of time.

Next, I got an excuse from school to travel to Africa with my grandmother. My teachers gave me all my homework assignments and told us where to either fax the homework or send it by e-mail. They also talked to JaJa about setting up a schedule so I would have time to complete my homework assignments and still have time to visit and see all the new sites. One of my homework assignments is to keep a written journal and take pictures to go with my journal.

Then JaJa bought our airplane tickets. We needed domestic airline tickets (tickets to fly inside the United States) to go round trip from where we live to the New York Kennedy International Airport. We also needed airline tickets to go from the New York Kennedy International Airport to

THE ADVENTURES OF JAJA AND JAMILA GOING TO AFRICA

Gambia in West Africa. JaJa requested a window seat for me and an aisle seat for herself. We were lucky. We got the seats we wanted on all the flights!

So we had our passports, visas and airplane tickets, but there were still other things to do before we could travel. We had to get our shots and medicine. I hate shots, but JaJa said I would have to get them or I wouldn't be able to go. She said the shots and medicine would protect me from getting sick and the Gambian government will not allow visitors to enter the country if they haven't gotten certain shots.

One more thing: we had to pack. JaJa helped me pack the right clothes to take on the trip. It is cool here, but it will be hot in Africa, so we packed my summer clothes, but I will wear my winter clothes while I am still in the United States.

AFRICA, HERE WE COME!

Finally the day arrived for us to leave for Africa. My parents drove JaJa and me to the airport to catch the plane to New York. When we arrived at our local airport, JaJa showed her identification at the airline check-in desk outside the terminal door leading to the airlines. The airline employee checked all of our luggage except our small carry-on bags. JaJa had to show her identification to get our boarding passes. The airline employee said I did not have to show my identification because I am underage and traveling with an adult.

We had to go through security screening before we could go to the airplane gate. We had to show our boarding passes and ID. We had to take off our shoes and coats and put them in a tray, then take out JaJa's laptop computer from its case and put it in another tray along with our purses and carry-on luggage.

After we passed through security, we walked a long way to find the departure gate. The departure area had quite a few people sitting around reading or watching the televisions mounted on the walls. Others were talking on their phones or listening to music or working on their computers. A few people were talking and some kids were playing games.

Finally we heard over the public address system that it was time to board the plane. We boarded the plane according to the order of our seat rows. Our seats were in the back row, so we were among the first group to board the plane. I was excited although I had been on a plane before. The plane was quite large and most of the seats were filled. From my window seat, I looked out as the plane took off. The ride was smooth as the plane climbed higher into the sky.

The flight to New York was going to take about two hours. When I got a little hungry, JaJa gave me a sandwich she brought from home. She said domestic airline flights rarely provide food any more. I smiled to myself because my mother always says JaJa keeps everything, including the kitchen sink, in her bag. I began on my homework, but dozed off. Before I knew it, the plane was preparing to land in New York.

When we arrived in New York City, we took an airport shuttle train to go from the domestic terminal to the international terminal to get the plane to Africa. This time we had to check our luggage inside the terminal. We had to show our tickets and our passports with our visas inside. That included me. We were asked for security reasons if anyone had given us anything to take on the plane and whether we had packed our own luggage. Then our luggage was checked. Next there was the security screening again! We showed our boarding passes, IDs and passports. Once again we had to take off our shoes and coats and put them in a tray, then take out JaJa's laptop computer and put it in a tray along with our purses and carry-on luggage. This was our second time going through a security screening in the same day. We were required to check in at least two hours before the scheduled flight time.

The check-in went quickly because not many passengers had arrived for our flight. We could relax until it was time to board the plane. We decided to have a snack in one of the many small restaurants in the airport food court. Afterwards, we decided to go to the duty free shops. The duty free shops sell clothes, cologne, purses and other things. JaJa said "duty free" means you do not have to pay import taxes on the things you buy there, so the items may be cheaper. We didn't buy anything. We just window shopped. I knew I wanted to spend my money in Africa.

When it was flight time, we went to the departure gate. Finally, we boarded the plane, which was much larger than the one we flew on to come to New York. Again JaJa had the aisle seat and I had the window seat. I wanted to see everything. It looked as if most of the seats were taken. There were many shades of people, speaking many languages, and wearing many different types of clothing. We saw quite a few children traveling with their parents.

Once the plane was in the air, we were allowed to watch movies, play music or turn on our computers. On the back of each seat was a small movie screen. JaJa checked the movies to see which were suitable for me. I was happy that one of them was a movie I really wanted to see. In the middle of the movie, the flight attendants served dinner. I put the movie on pause. I didn't like everything, but the dessert was yummy! After dinner, I turned the movie on again, but fell asleep before it ended. The flight was over eight hours long.

When I awakened, breakfast was being served. A short while later, the pilot announced we would be landing shortly. We were given immigration forms to fill out before we landed. JaJa filled out an immigration form for both of us. The form tells the officials in the country who we are, where we are from, where we will live while in the country, how long we will stay and why we are visitors. JaJa was also required to fill out a customs form, which tells officials whether banned items or items that should be taxed are being brought into the country. Most countries require this information from visitors.

TOUCH DOWN IN BANJUL!

The plane finally landed at the airport in Banjul, the capital city of Gambia in West Africa. I was really excited, but also very tired from the long plane rides. When the plane landed, many people clapped. JaJa said that passengers often applaud after a long flight or after a turbulent ride.

A bus was waiting for us as we walked down the steps from the plane. We rode a short distance to the terminal, and there we got in the immigration line. Then it was our turn to give the official our form and our passports, which he inspected to see if everything was in order. Next we went to the luggage pick up area, where many men were on hand to help us with our bags. We had one more stop to make in the airport. That was at the customs station. The customs official wanted to know what we were bringing into Gambia. We said we only had our regular pieces of luggage and we had nothing to report. The official inspected our visa and looked into one piece of our luggage. We were then free to pass to the next area, which meant we were officially visitors and guests of Gambia!

On the street outside the airport, the heat, the colorful sights, the fresh smell of the air surprised and excited me. People were everywhere! I could barely walk because I wanted to see everything. JaJa reminded me we would be in Africa for two and a half weeks, so I should pace myself.

OUR HOST FAMILY

JaJa's friend, Mr. Ly (pronounced Lee), met us at the airport. When Mr. Ly and JaJa saw each other, they began to laugh and gave each other a big hug. JaJa introduced me to him, and he gave me a big hug, too.

We walked to Mr. Ly's car, and the men who were helping with our luggage followed. They secured our luggage in the trunk and on top of Mr. Ly's compact car. While we were driving to the house, JaJa and Mr. Ly talked a lot, but all I could do was stare out the window.

We finally arrived at the house and we were met by all of Mr. Ly's family. Mr. Ly has three daughters, ages 19, 17 and 14. The two oldest girls attend vocational schools, but the youngest girl, who wants to be a doctor, goes to high school. We didn't meet Mrs. Ly because she works in another town and has their youngest child, a son, with her. Three boys live with the Ly family. They are the Lys' nephews, but everyone refers to them as the Lys' sons.

JaJa and I are living in the Ly family compound. It is a large, fenced-in piece of land with several buildings. The entrance to the compound is on a very busy street. The main house has four bedrooms, two baths, a living room, dining room, two-car garage and both an inside and an outside kitchen. It seems strange to have an inside kitchen because everyone cooks outside.

The inside of the family compound is mostly residential; however, the part that faces the street has several businesses. Uncle Amadou has a restaurant there where we sometimes eat breakfast or lunch. Breakfast is usually French bread, fruit, cheese or butter and tea. This is called a continental breakfast. I asked JaJa if we could have cereal. Later that day, Uncle Amadou (that is what JaJa and Mr. Ly said I should call him) drove us to a small grocery store where we purchased cereal and a few other things. The next day we put milk and bananas on the cereal and I was happy.

In the cool of the evening, we sit on the front patio that is paved with bright tiles. Uncle Amadou and his family usually eat a late dinner on the patio around eight o'clock. The food is served and eaten from a large, round platter. The family gathers in a circle so that everyone can reach the platter and everyone can eat at the same time. They may use spoons or eat with their hands. The children tease me when I eat with a spoon and try to get me to eat with my hands. Sometimes I try it, but mostly I eat with a spoon.

The dinner platter usually has vegetables with chicken, fish, lamb or a little beef. JaJa and I eat the fish very slowly because we are not used to fish with a lot of bones. Everyone in the family really likes fish heads, but JaJa and I don't! The Lys always offer us the fish heads anyway, then laugh when we say, "No, thank you!"

After dinner, Uncle Amadou's nephews make a strong, sweet green tea. Only the men drink the green tea. The young men offer JaJa tea, but she always says no, because the tea is too strong and keeps her awake at night.

JaJa doesn't make me eat only African food, but she wants me to try new foods to see if I like them. Anyway, I know JaJa will find foods that I enjoy. I did not see any of the fast food places I am used to -- like the burger, chicken and taco places. JaJa had told me that I should not expect to see them.

I have lots of children to play with. Mary, Uncle Amadou's middle daughter, told all of the children in the neighborhood I was coming and invited them to come meet me. Both boys and girls came by and brought balls and other toys and games. I didn't always understand what they were saying, but they smiled and made gestures, trying to help me understand. They taught me a few words and phrases in their language. They were so friendly to me! I felt very happy.

THE GARDEN

Uncle Amadou has a nice garden growing in his front yard. The garden covers about half of the yard. Every morning when I wake up, I see Uncle Amadou out of our window, walking and working in his garden. One afternoon I asked him if I could help him in the garden. He said yes, but I would have to get up early before the sun got too hot. The next morning, I got up early and put on a hat with a wide brim and some work gloves that Uncle Amadou gave me.

As we pulled weeds and watered the garden, Uncle Amadou told me about the different vegetables that he had planted. Some of the vegetables I knew and ate regularly, others were new to me. There were pumpkins, okra, tomatoes, onions, yams, and potatoes. Uncle Amadou explained that all the vegetables do not ripen at the same time. The yams are not the same as the sweet potatoes we know. They have a different color and taste.

There were also lemon and mango trees in the garden. Uncle Amadou showed me the special trees with leaves that can be used to make medicines. One day when JaJa was not feeling well, Uncle Amadou made tea for her from the leaves of one of the trees. Soon she was feeling just fine.

Uncle Amadou keeps the front gate closed because of wandering goats. Can you imagine goats coming into the garden and eating all the vegetables and the leaves off the lower branches of the fruit trees? Every morning when we are not going out on appointments and shopping, I help Uncle Amadou in the garden.

SHOPPING AT THE TOURIST MARKET

Uncle Amadou's oldest daughter is going to be a beautician. Everyone calls her Mama. School is out and she is taking JaJa and me to the large tourist market in the capital city, Banjul. Her middle sister, Mary, is going. Uncle Amadou will drive us to the market, but he has an appointment and can't wait to drive us back. Mama told him we would be just fine. We would take public transportation back home when we had finished shopping.

JaJa told me to stay close by her while we are in the market. She doesn't want me to get lost, and if there is a crowd, she doesn't want me to be frightened.

It took us about half an hour to get to the market. We arrived about 10 o'clock in the morning. There was so much to see: bright dresses for women and suits for men and children, lots of masks, colorful art pieces and jewelry everywhere.

JaJa seemed to know where she was going and what she wanted to see and purchase. The market women and men called out hello to us, trying to get our attention. They were vendors and wanted us to come to their booth to buy something. Sometimes JaJa would stop and sometimes she wouldn't.

Our first stop was at a booth with beautiful woven cloth. JaJa asked the man the price of the cloth. The man answered and JaJa unfolded the cloth and examined it. JaJa told me before we arrived at the market that there was no set price for any item. Prices had to be negotiated. JaJa explained to me that if she wanted something, she would pick up the item and examine it. She would ask the price, knowing that the vendor would say a very high price which they both knew was too expensive. She would say a price she knew was too low, but one she thought was closer to what she wanted to pay. JaJa and the man went back and forth about the price. This is called negotiating. Finally, they agreed on the price and JaJa paid the man for four beautiful pieces of woven cloth.

We continued walking in the market, buying dresses, suits, jewelry, bowls, baskets, and other beautiful things. Each time we bought an item, the negotiation process began again. After about the third or fourth vendor booth, other people who worked in the market started gathering around us and watching. A couple of times the crowd became very large and moved very close to us and everybody seemed to be talking at the same time. I became frightened. JaJa pulled me close to her and told the vendor she was bargaining with that she would have to leave because she could not think or hear herself. She said she was going home, but might come back another day.

The vendor didn't want to lose a sale so he asked the crowd to move back and lower their voices so that he could continue with JaJa. The group did as the vendor asked. Later JaJa explained that the other people were mostly vendors who wanted to do business with her, too.

THE ADVENTURES OF JAJA AND JAMILA GOING TO AFRICA

Because my grandmother is elderly, the vendors showed respect by offering her a stool to sit and rest. They also offered a cool drink of water or a cool soft drink. A vendor would send someone to get the drinks for her. JaJa said the vendors had very good business sense. They made their customers comfortable.

After a few hours, JaJa, Mama, Mary, and I stopped for lunch at a small outdoor cafe in the market. We had sandwiches and cool drinks.

I saw a doll and a tie-dye skirt set I liked. JaJa told me to try my hand at negotiating, but I was too shy. We bought some African print cloth so the tailor could make us some new clothes.

GETTING AROUND IN GAMBIA

Since we arrived in Gambia, our transportation has usually been by private car or taxi, but JaJa wanted me to see how most people get around in their daily lives. The first chance I had to experience public transportation came the day we went to the big tourist market.

We caught the mini van that most people ride. The vans are relatively inexpensive and come quite frequently. However, first you had to get to where the vans pick up passengers. We had to walk quite a way to find the van we needed. Each van has a driver and a young teenage boy who collects the fare and calls out the destination and the stops.

Every seat was taken in the van we rode. A lady next to JaJa had two small children with her. Children can sit on the seats if there are no customers, but children have to sit on their parents' laps if the van is full or the parents have to pay for them. Most parents are too poor to pay extra fares. JaJa reached over and took one of the children and held her on her lap. The mother seemed very relieved and said," Thank you, Mama." Most people call JaJa mama, grandmama or auntie. JaJa says that is a way of showing respect for an elder.

The people in the van were carrying things like big bags of rice, heavy buckets and food. When it was time to get out of the van, people would call out, and if they were in the back, they would pass their van fare to the front, and their change would be passed back.

I thought riding the mini van was fun. We rode the vans when we went to visit the schools. That is when I learned that getting around can be very tiring and a lot of work.

BUYING PRESENTS FOR EVERYONE

After my first experience at the big tourist market, Mama and Mary suggested I shop at a smaller tourist market. At first I said no, but JaJa said I might like the smaller market better. Besides, she said, I had to purchase gifts for my family and friends.

One bright afternoon while JaJa was at a meeting, Uncle Amadou drove Mama, Mary and me to a smaller market. I had a list of people to buy gifts for: my parents, little sister, grandfather, two best friends, my teachers and a few other people. I also wanted to buy some things for myself.

Uncle Amadou took us to the market, but stayed near the car. He said he didn't want to go shopping with the women. We laughed at him as we walked away. Later when we looked back, he was sitting in the car with the door open, talking to some of the market vendors and drinking tea. I don't think Uncle Amadou thinks of anyone as a stranger. He talks to everybody.

At the smaller tourist market, I saw a girl about my age making beaded necklaces and matching bracelets. They were so pretty. I wanted to buy some of them. She said if I waited about half an hour, she could make the beaded jewelry with my name or any name I wished.

I asked the girl the price of the jewelry and she asked how much I would pay. Then I realized I had to negotiate the price. Mama and Mary helped me. We finally agreed on a price. I ordered a necklace set for myself, one for my sister, and one for each of my best friends. They were going to love having their names on their beautiful beaded bracelets!

While we waited for the jewelry, we walked around looking for more gifts. We passed a booth with pretty tie-dyed, two-piece skirt and top sets. We looked through the clothes and found some in my size. The sets were in many colors, but I liked the blue one best. The blue matched the colors in my beaded necklace set. The vendor quoted me a very expensive price, but Mama and Mary said I must bargain. Finally we agreed on a price.

My father collects toy trains. I didn't find any toy trains, but I did see some really nice hand made toys that could go with his toy trains. I got a few for him. My grandfather plays chess and he has been giving me lessons. When I saw the chess set with the wonderful, hand-carved wooden African figures, I was so excited. I knew I wanted to get it for grandpa and our chess games together.

We saw several really nice wooden statues. For my mother, I chose a sculpture of a woman carrying a baby. I got it because it reminded me of a picture of my mother carrying me when I was a baby.

I bought some African dolls for my teachers. And I bought t-shirts and some small painted pictures to round off my gift list. We returned to the young girl, who, by then, had finished making the jewelry sets for me. I really liked all of them. We finished shopping and Uncle Amadou said goodbye to the vendors and drove us home.

WHAT'S A GOOD PRICE FOR FISH?

On another day, when JaJa was at a meeting, Uncle Amadou asked if I wanted to go grocery shopping with him and Mama. Of course, I said yes. We drove a long distance along the road that ran in front of the compound into the middle of the city.

When we arrived, we found the market very crowded. Mainly women and children were shopping for their daily meal, just as we were. Almost every shopper had a plastic basket like the ones in grocery stores. As we walked by, many of the market women called out what they were selling and their prices.

Uncle Amadou would stop to inspect fish or negotiate the price of some of the foods. With a straight face, he would sometimes say to me, "Jamila, what do you think? Is this a good price for this fish?" I would act as if I knew by getting close to the fish and looking at it. Then I would say, "Yes, Uncle. It's a pretty good price." Later when we had completed our food shopping and were back in the car, Uncle Amadou, Mama and I would have a good laugh about the game Uncle Amadou played with me. We dropped off all the food items so Miss Abby, the cook, could start preparing dinner.

THE TAILOR SHOP ON THE FRONT PORCH

JaJa brought several patterns with her to take to the tailor to have suits made while she was in Gambia. One day we went shopping in the area where there are many fabric stores. Guess what? Yes, in order to get the lowest price we had to negotiate! Because JaJa was buying several pieces of fabric, she was able to get a very good price. Then we were off to the tailor shops that JaJa likes to use.

The first tailor we visited has a wife and two children, an eight-year-old boy and a little girl about six months old. They live in a small apartment with a living room, bedroom and a bathroom. The cooking area is outside in the back yard.

The tailor shop is on the family's small front porch. The tailor works outside to be sure of having enough light, because often the electricity goes off. The sewing machine, like so many sewing machines in West Africa, is an old foot pedal machine which doesn't require electricity. Besides the sewing machine and his stool, the tailor has a small cutting board where he lays out his designs. JaJa uses several tailors, but she says this one is her favorite. She would have him make all her clothes, but she is only there for a short while and he can only sew so much.

The tailor took our measurements and discussed the styles we wanted and when they would be completed. Lastly, JaJa and the tailor negotiated the price of the items and we left to go to another tailor.

There is another small tailor shop not too far from the first tailor where mostly young men work. JaJa likes the fancy embroidery work they do, but she says the shop is not well kept or very clean. The young men don't seem to sweep or mop often. JaJa was afraid her fabric would get dirty, but she decided to give them another try. We looked in their books and found three beautiful outfits she liked and one for me. The tailor who was assigned to her took our measurements. JaJa gave them the fabric and they negotiated the price for the clothes.

Lately, JaJa has been using the tailor across the street from Uncle Amadou's compound. This tailor has a couple of young men working for him. This shop is so convenient when it comes to extra fittings or if changes are needed. JaJa decided to have several new outfits made at this tailoring shop as well.

It was so strange to me to see that most of the people sewing were men. I used to think that only women used sewing machines. All of our clothes turned out beautifully and JaJa was very pleased.

WATCH OUT FOR MOSQUITOES!

Malaria is a serious problem in many African countries, including Gambia. The disease is caused by a parasite that is transmitted by mosquitoes. You get malaria when infected mosquitoes bite you. The infected bug can make you very sick with a fever and other symptoms. People from areas where malaria is not common are more vulnerable to the disease because they have no immunity. JaJa and I had to take medication to protect us against malaria before we went to Africa and while we were there.

In each bedroom at Uncle Amadou's house there is a white net over the bed. Everyone in the house sleeps under the bed nets every night so mosquitoes can't bite them. JaJa and I also burned mosquito candles to ward off the bugs, and before we went to bed, we used mosquito repellent.

At night we would get into bed and tuck the net under the sides of the mattress. The only problem was sometimes I would wake up and forget where I was and the bed net would frighten me. Each time that happened, JaJa would awaken and help me get settled in again.

Everyone - who can afford to buy one - sleeps under a mosquito net. The nets are usually made of a white, gauze-like material. The net, which is attached to a hook in the ceiling, is small at the top, but pleated and very wide at the bottom. Some nets are big enough to cover a very large bed. Sometimes the net is very large and it hangs along the side of the bed. At night when we had to get up, we would untuck the net then retucked it when we returned to bed.

GAMBIAN FRIENDS

JaJa has been to Gambia several times, and she met some of her Gambian friends when they were in the United States. So we always had visitors in the evenings and we also went out to dinner at her friends' homes.

Uncle Amadou asks the cook to prepare extra food whenever JaJa comes to visit. He said she is so popular and he knows everybody will be coming to visit. He told me that in Africa, visitors who come at mealtime are always invited to eat with the family.

Whenever we went to visit JaJa's friends, there were always many of children to play with. I liked most of the children, but a few of the big kids would take our ball. The other children my age said the big boys liked to play a game called soccer. I didn't know the game. One day Uncle Amadou was watching soccer on TV. He taught me some of the rules of the game. He said it's very popular in most of the world except a few places like the United States. He said it will probably be popular soon in the United States with so many big stars of the game playing on U.S. teams.

LIGHTS ON, LIGHTS OFF

The electricity service is quite poor in Gambia. Several days a week the lights go off. That means we could not watch TV, listen to the radio (unless it was battery operated), use the hair dryer or use an electric iron to press our clothes. The really big problem for me and JaJa was that the ceiling fan didn't work, and it was hot in our room.

Everyone seemed to take the lack of electricity in stride. If the lights were off in the evenings, we would light candles to eat by or sit and talk or play games. The problem was the children had to do their homework by candle light. I did my homework during the day since I was on vacation.

When the lights were off, Uncle Amadou used a battery-operated radio to listen to the local and world news. The children wanted to listen to music on the radio, but they knew their father would say no. The radio was used only for news and emergencies. Batteries are very expensive.

The children who lived nearby would come over in the evening whether the lights were on or not. If the lights were on, we usually looked at television, and if the lights were out, we would fix our hair or play games. Either way, we had fun and laughed a lot.

There were always candles in the living room, bedrooms and bathroom. They knew JaJa and I needed more light. JaJa said everyone was very considerate of us and she really appreciated it.

ONE OCEAN, TWO COASTS

One beautiful day, Uncle Amadou and his daughters, Mama and Mary, took me to the beach. Ashiea, the youngest girl, had not gotten home from school when we left. It was her late school day. The beach was along the Atlantic Ocean on the African coast. Wow! I realized that I had been swimming in the Atlantic Ocean before, but then I was at a beach in New Jersey - on the U.S. coast of the Atlantic! The waves seemed a little higher than I was used to. I can swim, but I usually swim in a pool at our local recreation center.

We had to stay close to the shore. Uncle Amadou would let me go out into the ocean only a few feet. He said if anything happened to me, he would have to run away and hide from JaJa because she is so fierce. We all just laughed.

We brought blankets and lay on the beach to dry out after playing in the water for quite a while. We bought cool drinks from a vendor selling snacks on the beach.

The day was so warm and beautiful. There was not a cloud in the sky. I guess because it was the middle of a school and work day, not many people were on the beach.

MS. MARIAMME TAKES US TO SCHOOL

We visited several schools. The group JaJa is representing sent a nice young lady to be our guide. Her name is Ms. Mariamme. We asked her whether the Lys' compound was difficult to locate. She said it wasn't difficult. She knew the area because she was born and grew up in a nearby village.

We left the house around nine o'clock in the morning to begin our school visit. We caught the little mini van that most people ride. We had to take two mini vans to get to the school. When we got off the second mini van, we had to walk for what seemed like a long time. It was difficult to walk because there were no sidewalks and we had to walk in sand.

When we arrived, we found the school yard very large and sandy with the school buildings in the middle. JaJa was there to meet two children, a sister, 13 years old, and her brother, 11 years old, who had been offered scholarships by her group. Their names are Akena and Olu.

All the students at this school wore uniforms of red pants or skirts and white shirts or blouses with red and white checkered collars. All school children in Gambia seem to wear uniforms. Each school has different uniform colors that are very well known by people in the community. Anyone passing the children on foot or by car, van or bus can easily recognize which school the students attend. Children often walk a long way to attend school.

We went to the administration office (similar to the principal's office). JaJa introduced herself, Ms. Mariamme and me. The administrator was very interested in JaJa's organization. JaJa told the administrator about her group's goals. Then she asked about Akena and Olu's progress and whether their school fees were being paid on time.

As the administrator talked, JaJa was writing in her notebook. She was taking notes for the report she had to make when we returned home. After the report, the administrator called her assistant into her office and asked her to take us to Akena and Olu's classes.

The classrooms were very crowded. The assistant said there were fifty-five students per classroom, with each classroom having one teacher and an assistant.

The children were excused from class to visit with JaJa. The assistant introduced the children to us and JaJa talked to them a while, asking them about their school work. She then took their pictures and some pictures with me, the administrator and our guide. The guide took pictures of JaJa and the children, then one with me, JaJa and the children. It was fun being with all the adults and the students. After a while, we left the school and returned to Uncle Amadou's house, taking two mini vans and walking a lot.

By the time we arrived at Uncle Amadou's, we were all very hungry. For breakfast, we had eaten only a small piece of bread, some fruit and tea. We were ready for lunch. We asked Ms. Mariamme to stay for lunch and she did. After lunch, it was nap time for JaJa and me. Ms. Mariamme left, saying she would see us the next day.

During the next few days, I went to three other schools with JaJa and Ms. Mariamme. I had to be careful to say Ms. Mariamme because in Africa, children do not call adults by their first name alone. They have to show respect.

SHOW AND TELL

When I get back to school, I will have lots of things for our regular show and tell. Also, I will have so much for our African American History Month display, especially the dolls I bought for myself that are dressed in traditional African clothes and beautiful head dresses.

I will also take my necklace and bracelet set that the young girl in the market made for me. I can wear my two-piece blue tie-dyed skirt set. I will ask my father if I can take his toys to show as well. They are so nice. Perhaps my grandfather will let me take his chess set, and I will ask my mother to let me take her statue. I will make a poster with my photos. Wow! What a great presentation for show and tell!

TIME TO GO HOME

The day before it was time to leave Gambia to go home, JaJa told me we had to be sure we were ready to leave. We went to all the tailor shops to pick up our new clothes and they were ready! We were really happy about that.

When we returned to the house, we had to gather all the things we brought -- our clothes, toiletries, and books. We also had to gather all the things we bought. That was a lot. We folded all of our clothes and packed them in our luggage. JaJa checked to make sure we had our passports and tickets. She laid out the clothes we were going to wear on the plane.

That evening Miss Abby, the cook, prepared JaJa's favorite food, chicken yassa with rice. It's my favorite African food, too. After the meal, everyone in the household gathered around and told us how much they would miss us and that they hoped we would come back soon to visit them. It was so nice and I was a little sad to be leaving, but I really missed my family and friends. We had this celebration in the evening because all of the children would be in school the following day and would be unable to say goodbye.

That night JaJa and I talked about our trip. She wanted to know if I had enjoyed myself and what I liked best. I told her I was really glad that she had let me come with her. The best part of all was that I felt free. I could go out in the yard and over to the other children's houses and not be worried or afraid. There were people everywhere. Uncle Amadou said they were watching over us. The children were very friendly and nice to me. Also I liked visiting the schools. I even liked shopping at the smaller market.

DEAR JOURNAL: THE LONG TRIP BACK

I am back home. On the first day back, all I could do was sleep. The trip back was so long. Before leaving Gambia, we had to go back through immigration and customs. Before we arrived in the United States, we had to fill out a card for customs. Once we arrived in New York, we had to go through immigration and customs. First we had to get our luggage. Then we went to the line for customs, where the official asked JaJa about our trip. We opened our luggage for his inspection.

When this process was finished, we went through the double doors and we were officially back in the United States! We caught the airport shuttle train from the international terminal to the domestic terminal to catch our plane back home.

The remainder of my homework will be a breeze because I have so much to write about and so many pictures to show everyone. Maybe JaJa will take me on another wonderful trip with her. I sure hope so.

KEIRA PRESS ORDER FORM

Forward Your Order to: Ship To:

Keira Press LLC   Name _____

P.O. Box 815   Address _____

Joliet, IL 60434   City _____

                        Email address _____

                        Phone _____

ITEM

The Adventures of JaJa and Jamila Going to Africa

Quantity	Price Per Book	Shipping and Handling Cost	
__ 1 to 5 Books	$7.95	$.25 per book plus $1.00	$_____
__ 6 to 29 Books	$7.50	$.25 per book plus $2.00	$_____
__ 30 to 49 Books	$6.95	$.25 per book plus $3.00	$_____
__ 50 to 99 Books	$6.25	$.25 per book plus $4.00	$_____
__ over 100 Books	$5.25	Only $.25 per book	$_____

Illinois residents please add 8.5% (.085) for sales tax $_____

                                                    TOTAL $_____

Please make all checks or money orders out to: **KEIRA PRESS LLC**
Delivery will be made in 3-6 weeks.

Thank you for your order.

KEIRA PRESS ORDER FORM

Forward Your Order to: Ship To:

Keira Press LLC

P.O. Box 815

Joliet, IL 60434

Name _____

Address _____

City _____

Email address _____

Phone _____

ITEM

The Adventures of JaJa and Jamila Going to Africa

Quantity	Price Per Book	Shipping and Handling Cost	
__ 1 to 5 Books	$7.95	$.25 per book plus $1.00	$_____
__ 6 to 29 Books	$7.50	$.25 per book plus $2.00	$_____
__ 30 to 49 Books	$6.95	$.25 per book plus $3.00	$_____
__ 50 to 99 Books	$6.25	$.25 per book plus $4.00	$_____
__ over 100 Books	$5.25	Only $.25 per book	$_____

Illinois residents please add 8.5% (.085) for sales tax $_____

TOTAL $_____

Please make all checks or money orders out to: **KEIRA PRESS LLC**
Delivery will be made in 3-6 weeks.

Thank you for your order.